It's fun to draw
Pirates

Mark Bergin

Sky Pony Press
New York

Author:

Mark Bergin was born in Hastings, England. He has illustrated an award-winning series and written over twenty books. He has done many book designs, layouts, and storyboards in many styles including cartoon for numerous books, posters, and advertisements. He lives in Bexhill-on-sea with his wife and three children.

HOW TO USE THIS BOOK:
Start by following the numbered splats on the left-hand page. These steps will ask you to add some lines to your drawing. The new lines are always drawn in red so you can see how the drawing builds from step to step. Read the "You can do it!" splats to learn about drawing and coloring techniques you can use.

Sky Pony Press books may be purchased in bulk at special discounts for sales promotion, corporate gifts, fund-raising, or educational purposes. Special editions can also be created to specifications. For details, contact the Special Sales Department, Sky Pony Press, 307 West 36th Street, 11th Floor, New York, NY 10018 or info@skyhorsepublishing.com.

Sky Pony® is a registered trademark of Skyhorse Publishing, Inc.®, a Delaware corporation.

Visit our website at www.skyponypress.com.

10 9 8 7 6 5 4 3 2 1

Manufactured in China, June 2014
This product conforms to CPSIA 2008

Library of Congress Cataloging-in-Publication Data is available on file.

Cover illustrations credit Mark Bergin

Print ISBN: 978-1-62914-612-6

Contents

Barnacle Boris

1 Start with an oval for the head, and add a line and ears.

2 Add a hat, nose, mouth, eyes, and eyebrows.

3 Draw in the body. Add two lines for the waistcoat.

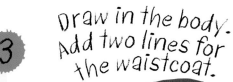

4 Draw in the trousers, belt, and feet.

Splat-a-fact!
Pirates used guns and swords as weapons.

5 Draw in arms holding a pistol and a sword.

you can do it!

Use crayons to create various textures, then paint over it with watercolor paint. Use a felt-tip marker for the lines.

5

sharktooth Jack

 1 Draw in the head shape with dots for the eyes. Add a line for the headscarf.

 **you can do it!**
Use a crayon to draw the clouds. To add texture paint over with watercolor paint. Use a felt-tip marker for the lines.

 **2** Draw in the eyebrows and mouth. Add dots for stubble and a knotted headscarf.

3 Draw in the body.

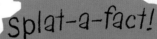 **splat-a-fact!**
Pirates buried their treasure on desert islands.

4 Add ragged trousers and legs.

5 Draw in the arms and hands. Draw in the spade.

Redbeard

1 Draw in the head shape. Add a line for the headscarf.

2 Draw in the beard and eye patch. Add dots for the eye and mouth.

3 Draw in a circle for the body. Add a belt and waistcoat.

4 Draw in two arms and a lit match.

you can do it!
Use a graphite pencil for the lines and colored inks to add color.

5 Draw in ragged trousers, and add the feet.

Splat-a-fact!
Pirate ships had cannons to shoot at their enemies with.

Scurvy Jim

1 Draw in the head shape. Add a line for the headscarf.

Splat-a-fact!
Pirate treasure is kept in a wooden chest.

2 Draw a dot for the eye. Add the mouth, ear, hair, and knotted headscarf.

3 Draw in the body shape, and add a belt and waistcoat.

4 Draw in the arms carrying a treasure chest and sword.

5 Draw in ragged trousers, and add the feet.

You can do it!
Use a black felt-tip marker for the lines. Add color using oil pastels and draw scribbly lines so the color looks more interesting.

squid lips Sid

1 Start with the head shape, and draw a line for the headscarf.

2 Add dots for eyes. Draw in the eyebrows, an ear, and the knotted headscarf.

3 Add the body, arms, and hands.

4 Draw in the torn trousers and feet.

5 Draw in the belt and broom.

splat-a-fact!
Scrubbing the decks
was a pirate
punishment.

starboard Steve

1 Start with the head shape. Draw in a line for the headscarf.

2 Draw in the eyes, mouth, and hair. Add an ear, an earring, and a knotted headscarf.

3 Add a box-shaped body and two lines for the waistcoat.

Splat-a-fact!
"X" marks the spot on a treasure map where the treasure is buried.

4 Draw in torn trousers, and add feet.

5 Draw in the arms holding a treasure map. Add a neckerchief.

Monkey

 1 Draw two overlapping circles for the head. Add the hairline.

 **2** Draw in dots for the eyes and nostrils. Add a mouth and ears.

 3 Draw in the body. Add a headscarf.

you can do it!
Cut out strips of corrugated cardboard for the rope and glue down torn tissue paper for the background.

4 Draw in torn trousers, and add the monkey's legs and feet.

5 Add arms and a long tail. Draw circles for fingers.

Captain Clunk

1 Start by cutting out this shape for the pirate's jacket. Glue down.

2 Cut out the face shape. Glue down. Use a felt-tip marker to draw in buttons, hair, a nose, and an eye patch.

you can do it!

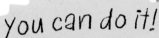

As you cut out each shape from colored paper or tin foil, glue it down.

3 Cut out the pirate's hat and beard from black paper. Glue down. Cut out a boot and a peg leg from brown paper. Glue down.

4 Cut out the sword from tin foil and glue down. Cut out hands and glue down. Cut a crutch from brown paper and glue down.

18

Splat-a-fact!
Some pirates had
wooden legs.

Sophie Storm

1 Start with a circle for the head. Add a nose, mouth, and eyes.

2 Draw in a hat and hair.

3 Draw in a box-shaped body. Add sleeves.

you can do it!
Use a brown felt-tip marker for the lines and add color with colored crayons.

4 Draw in circles for the hands holding a sword and dagger. Add belts and buckles.

Splat-a-fact!
Sometimes girls were pirates, too!

5 Add the trousers and the feet.

20

One-eyed John

1 Start with an oval for the head. Add ears.

you can do it!
Use a felt-tip marker for the lines. Add ink washes then add a second colored ink on top of an area that is still wet for extra effects.

2 Draw in a headscarf. Add a nose, a dot for the eye, an eye patch, and a dagger between his teeth.

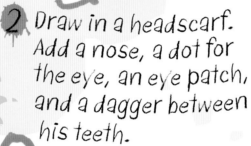

3 Draw in a box-shaped body. Add a waistcoat and buckle.

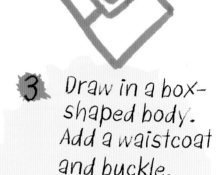

4 Draw in the arms with circles for the hands. Add a pistol.

Splat-a-fact!
Pirates wore eye patches and headscarves.

5 Draw in ragged trousers, and add the feet.

Pete the Plank

1 Start by drawing in the head shape with a line for the headscarf.

2 Add a mouth, an ear, eyebrows, and dots for eyes. Draw in a knotted headscarf.

3 Draw in the body. Add a belt and buckle.

splat-a-fact!
Pirates climbed the "rigging"—ropes that controlled the mast.

you can do it!
Use a brown felt-tip marker for the outlines and color in with different felt-tip markers.

4 Draw in ragged trousers, and add the feet.

5 Draw in the arms and hands. Add stripes to the trousers and shirt.

24

sharkbait George

1 Start with the head shape. Add a line for the headscarf.

2 Draw in the knotted headscarf. Add an ear, mouth, and an arrow-shaped closed eye.

3 Add the ragged trousers.

4 Draw in the arms, with one holding up a telescope.

you can do it!
Use a felt-tip marker for the lines and then add color with watercolor paints. Dab on more color with a sponge to add texture.

5 Draw in a waistcoat, buckle, and belt. Add the legs, feet, and a cannonball.

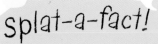

Splat-a-fact!
Telescopes helped pirates see into the distance.

26

Gunpowder Billy

1 Start with an oval for the head. Add a line for the headscarf.

Splat-a-fact!

Pirates attacked enemy ships and kept much of the loot.

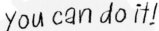

2 Add a mouth, nose, hair, and dots for the eyes. Draw in the knotted headscarf.

3 Draw in the body shape.

you can do it!

Use a felt-tip marker for the lines. Add color using chalky pastels. Use your fingers to blend the colors.

4 Draw in the ragged trousers, and add legs and feet.

5 Draw in the arms, a treasure chest, and a bag of loot.

Captain Black

 Start with a square-shaped head. Add the shape of the hat.

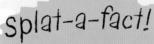 Draw in the nose, hair, and beard.

you can do it!

Using crayons to create texture, paint over it with watercolor paint. Use a felt-tip marker for the lines.

Splat-a-fact!

Some pirates had hooks for hands.

3 Draw in one eye, an eye patch, and a mouth. Add a box-shaped body and an "X" to the hat.

 Draw in the jacket details: buttons and button holes. Add buckle. Draw in boots.

5 Draw in sleeves with big cuffs. Add one hand with a sword and one with a hook.

Index